Change your
Change your

\- John C. Maxwell

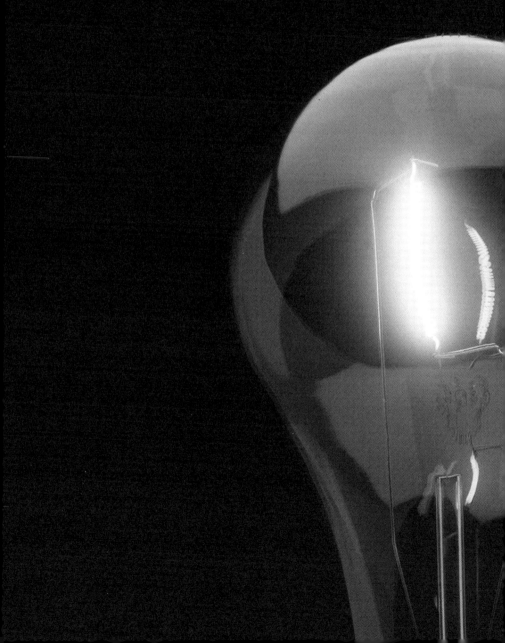

FOREWORD

O ccasionally, you read something that hits home and makes you think, "Wow! That really resonates…it's relevant and important!" Reading thi handbook was one of those times for me.

Well before I got to the last page of *180 Ways to Effectively Deal With Change*, knew that Laurie Calzada had hit a home run. Her insights into real-world organizational issues – as well as her candor and practicality in dealing with people – are reflected throughout this timely work about a truly timeless subject

In today's workplace, because we're often so busy just holding our own (and holding *on* to the status quo), we miss far too many opportunities to step "out of the box" – to see how we can improve things, help others navigate through changing times, and take the lead on advancing forward to a better tomorrow. Those opportunities need to be seized rather than squandered. And that's what this book is all about.

Two facts are undeniable: (1) Change is the key to survival and success, and (2) Change isn't going away. And regardless of whether you are an individual contributor or hold a leadership position, this handbook will help you effectively deal with *both* of those realities.

ERIC HARVEY
President and Founder
The WALK THE TALK® Company

180 Ways to Effectively Deal With Change

Get Over It! Get With It! Get To It!

Laurie Calzada

DEDICATED TO

Angeles and Austin…the biggest change in my entire life!
You help me strive every day to be a better mother and a better person.

THANK YOU TO

my wonderful staff at Sharp Approach and Dynamic Approach for
challenging and encouraging me to make the necessary changes
to cultivate growth within our lives and organizations.

And a very special thank you to
Steve Ventura and Michelle Sedas
for your encouragement, insight, and expertise to
make this become a reality and a success.

The  Company

Helping organizations achieve success through Ethical
Leadership and Values-Based Business Practices
www.walkthetalk.com

180 Ways to Effectively Deal With Change

Copyright © 2006 by Laurie Calzada and Walk The Talk
Published by Walk the Talk

Design: Tim Steele
Edited by: Michelle Sedas

Printed in the United States of America

ISBN 1-885228-80-5

9 781885 228802

TABLE OF CONTENTS

INTRODUCTION

Like it or not, life has become a whirlwind of change. Our society moves at a pace that far exceeds any other time in history...

constantly changing...
constantly moving...
constantly growing...
constantly progressing.

Change is a reality in today's workplace. It can be a very POSITIVE thing when it is implemented effectively, efficiently, and with encouragement. Unfortunately, that doesn't happen as often as it could...or should. As a result, we're often left with "a bad taste in our mouths" when required to do things differently. But regardless of how change is implemented – regardless of how we feel about it – change is not changing. It's here to stay.

If you change the way you look at things, the things you look at change.
— Wayne Dyer

So, we all need to deal with it...we all need to **GET OVER IT!** Instead of lamenting, each of us needs to look at all the *positive* things around us that are changing and evolving.

Fact is, change is the key ingredient for organizational survival and individual success, so we all need to **GET WITH IT!** If an organization and its people are not willing to change *how* they do things, *when* they do them, and *who* does them, then their chances of survival are slim. Remember that today is not the same as yesterday, and tomorrow will be different than today.

Because we're human (i.e. "creatures of habit"), we ALL tend to resist change at various times and in various degrees. And that is something we must learn to overcome. This book will help you do just that. In the pages that follow, you'll find tips and techniques for managing the challenges of change in your professional and personal lives...regardless of whether you are the receiver or the instigator of change. So, **GET TO IT!**

In the first two parts of this book, you will find useful ideas for dealing with changes that impact you directly. In part three, those who must inspire others and lead them through the impacts of change will find specific strategies for increasing its acceptance and techniques for implementing it more effectively.

Regardless of whether you like it or not, remember that the ship is still going to leave the dock – with you or without you.

So, let's look at how to make sure that you are on board...

REACTING TO CHANGE IS YOUR CHOICE

You can choose to ignore it,
or you can choose to recognize it.
You can choose to tolerate it,
or you can choose to embrace it.
You can choose to avoid it,
or you can choose to implement it.
You can choose to hate it,
or you can choose to love it.
You can choose to follow it,
or you can choose to lead it.
You can choose to deny it,
or you can choose to accept it.
You can choose to cover it,
or you can choose to expose it.
You can choose to run from it,
or you can choose to face it.

You choose!

— **Laurie Calzada**

GET OVER IT:
CHANGING YOUR PERCEPTION

D o you embrace change? Or do you hate it? If you hate change, do you only dislike the aspects of change that you can't control? To be sure, change may not always be your decision. Sometimes you will be the initiator of change, but more often you are probably the one told to make it happen. If you view change as a chore, you'll be much less likely to willingly accept it and use it to your benefit. So, try changing your perception. View it as an adventure. Find creative and adventurous ways to implement change in your life and your organization.

> *Begin with the end in mind.*
> - Stephen Covey

Think of change as something POSITIVE. You can't always choose the situations you face, but you CAN choose the way you respond to those situations. Nobody can force you to feel down on your luck, and no one can force you to be upbeat. Both come from the attitude that YOU decide to have at any given moment. After all, self-motivation is not genetic. It's not some inherent characteristic that some have and others don't. It's merely a CHOICE. Is change something negative for you? If so, choose to **CHANGE YOUR PERCEPTION**!

Here are some helpful perception-changing tips and techniques that you can start implementing now...

1 FOCUS ON PAST RESULTS. Write down several benefits of change that you have experienced in the last year. Review your list periodically as a reminder of how change has been beneficial for you.

2 Force yourself to use at least one new technology or computer feature a month. You will become more accepting of change, and you will become more efficient in the process.

3 STRETCH YOURSELF...literally. When you feel stressed or tired, get up and stretch your body. Stretched muscles release oxygen to your brain.

4 If you are upset about a required change you are facing, wait 24 hours. If you are still upset, then talk to your boss about it. If you're no longer upset about it, then it wasn't worth getting upset about initially.

Today is the tomorrow that you worried about yesterday.

5 When you are having difficulties accepting change, try to change your perception by focusing on your own personal goals. You need to determine how you define your own level of success. DON'T COMPARE YOURSELF TO OTHERS. Set your goals and write them down with a target date.

> *Whether you think that you CAN, or that you CAN'T...you're right!*
> - Henry Ford

Review your list the last day of every month. Add new goals to the list, and mark off the ones that you have completed. You can accomplish anything if you are willing to focus on the goal and not worry about the hurdles that you may have to jump over to get there.

6 Be Gumby—BE FLEXIBLE. The basis of all change is flexibility. Buy yourself a Gumby doll or some similar object. When you start getting frustrated with the change that is occurring, play with it. Pull its head...twist its legs...bend it in half...Don't worry; it won't break, just like you will not break going through change. It will help you get through the frustrating times of change, and it will help you realize that by being flexible, you cannot break.

7 DREAMS MEAN CHANGE. You can't have a dream that doesn't require change in your life. Let the power of what you want to become be greater than the fear you have of becoming it. Therefore, develop a *Dreams To-Do List*. Write out your dreams in as much detail as possible. Describe them as though they have already happened. Now, list the changes you'll probably need to make in order to achieve them.

If you stop changing, you stop dreaming.

8 Give yourself a break. When change is happening at a pace that is too overwhelming, take a day or two off from the situation to concentrate on other things. Come back with a fresh mind and a new attitude.

9 Practice getting out of your comfort zone. Move your watch to a different wrist for a week. It will feel odd the first day or so, but by the end of the week, it will feel normal.

If life's too comfortable, it might be time for a change.

10 Go with the flow. Remember that you don't always have to take the wheel when change is being implemented, but you better make sure you are on the same ship, or you may be left floating in the water. When in doubt, ask for clarification about the expectations for your role aboard the *Change Boat.*

11 CHANGE YOUR LIGHTBULB! If it seems that things are getting a little "dim" in a time of change, then increase your wattage. Don't sit in a dark and gloomy room. Bring in a lightbulb from home, or print off a picture of a lightbulb, and write "Change My Wattage" on it with a marking pen. Place it somewhere in your office or work area as a constant reminder to brighten your perspective.

12 Make an *Obstacles to Change Binder.* Eliminate those things that get in the way of choosing and implementing positive change. Keep a binder with a list of tasks, meetings, habits, or reports that you would like to stop doing. These are items that are nonproductive and tend to waste your time. Review them every week to make sure you are NOT doing them.

13 Remember...focus on growth, NOT current circumstances. The next time you are troubled by a pending change, take a moment to write down all of the personal growth opportunities the change might afford you. Review your list several times and then return to the tasks at hand.

If you aren't happy, only YOU can change it.

14 Often we resist change due to a perception of risk. Lower your resistance by having a contingency plan. Never go into a major crisis or implement a major change without Plan A and a contingency Plan B. Write out your backup plan, place it in a folder, and lock it away in a drawer. Hopefully you will never need it, but if you do, you've got it.

15 During changing times, people have a tendency to perceive things differently. And sometimes they will hear what they want to hear. Remember, IT'S NOT ALWAYS WHAT YOU SAY, BUT HOW YOU SAY IT. Next time you get a negative reaction from something you said, ask them to repeat back to you "how" and "what" you just said. You may be amazed at the interpretation, and it will help you realize how you are being perceived, and perhaps how you perceive others.

16 Decide to view change as a challenge, not a chore. Instead of looking at change as something that you "have to do," try telling yourself that it's something you "want to do." It will help you focus on the tasks at hand, and you will be surprised along the way to find other things that need improving. There is true magic in the **POWER OF POSITIVE THINKING**.

17 When you feel overwhelmed by changing circumstances, say out loud, "I will survive whatever happens today."

18 GET OUT OF YOUR BOX BY PUTTING THINGS INTO YOUR BOX! If you live your life within artificial and limiting boundaries that you have set for yourself, you may miss many great opportunities that await you. So, get out your box cutter, get a small cardboard box, and cut a slot in the top of the box. On white index cards, write what you think fits inside of your box comfortably, and put the cards in the box. Then take yellow index cards, write things that do not fit in your box, and tape them to the side of the box. Make it a weekly goal to change one of your yellow cards and place it in the box.

19 North, South, East, and West...Which direction are you going? If you are not sure, buy a compass. Put a symbol for each direction. North = On Track; South = Off Track; East = Losing Focus; West = Getting Refocused. At the conclusion of each day, turn the needle of the compass in the direction that you feel you headed that day.

20 If you don't agree with the change that is being implemented, and you have no control, try writing down five positive things that will come out of the change for you personally. Review the list every day before you leave for work.

21 First reactions don't have to be your lasting reactions. Always keep in mind that change can cultivate growth, opportunity, and advancement... for YOU! When you feel that sudden feeling of "Ugh—More change," remind yourself to:

1) Hold your tongue.
2) Suspend your judgments.
3) Gather information.
4) Clarify expectations and objectives.

22 Celebrate all your worries about change! Create a *Worry Jar*, and each time you have a worry, write it down and place it in the jar. Take time every week to open the jar and worry about all your worries. When you get tired of worrying about something, remove it from the jar. Over time, you'll have fewer and fewer worries.

Worries don't change tomorrow, actions do!

23 STOP being a creature of BAD habits. There are moments in life when habits are a positive reinforcement of who you are and what you do. However, during times of change, resistance habits need to be broken. You cannot change habits overnight. It takes at least 21 days. So, make a *Calendar of Change*. At the commencement of the change, count 21 days out and draw a large red circle around that day. Then consciously work to change or eliminate the counterproductive habit. As each day ends, place a large red X in that day. Once you reach your red circle, the old habit will likely be a thing of the past.

> *Definition of Insanity: Doing the same thing over and over, and expecting a different result.*
>
> - Albert Einstein

24 Change is like basketball. It's okay if you take a shot and miss, but you can't score a point unless you are willing to take the shot. Many of us stand on the sidelines of change...nothing risked...nothing gained. Practice change readiness by putting a toy basketball hoop in your department. When team members have new ideas, allow them to take a shot at the basket. Assess the benefits, think long term, consider your goals, aim, and shoot.

25 TAKE RESPONSIBILITY for your job and your career. If you spend your life pointing the finger and blaming others for where you are (or aren't) in your life, then you give up control of your own destiny. Remember, whenever you point a finger at someone else, three of your fingers are pointing back at YOU!

Manage change—don't let it manage you.

26 Rather than complaining, choose to increase your cooperation and your credibility in times of change. DON'T BE THE SQUEAKY WHEEL! **NO ONE WANTS TO OIL YOU**. Eventually people will cover their ears. Or worse yet, they'll start squeaking like you.

27 Negativity breeds negativity. It is much easier to think negative thoughts about change versus positive ones. That is human nature. So, stop being human for a moment! Don't believe the negative. If someone states, "You probably **can't** finish the project by Friday," respond by saying, "I **will** finish the project by Friday." Amazing the difference one little word makes!

Success is never definite, and failure is never final.

28 STOP LOOKING IN THE REARVIEW MIRROR! Don't focus on what you are leaving behind, but rather where you are going. So many people look behind them thinking, "I wish I could've...would've...should've..." Instead, say, "I can...I will...I must..."

29 USE THE POWER OF 10%. So many times we fail to implement change because we try to accomplish too much, too fast. Let's say that you want to be a better golfer, and you currently shoot a 90. Don't aim for par, rather tell yourself that you want to decrease your score by 10%. Therefore, set a goal of 81. Once you have reached that goal, keep setting goals of 10% until you achieve par. You can use the *Power of 10%* approach in many different areas of life, such as reaching sales quotas, increasing customer service calls, setting yearly goals, losing weight, etc.

30 TAKE A HIKE! As the pace of our society continues to increase, it adds a deeper complexity to change in our lives. We live in the fastest-paced society in the world. We live in it, and it lives in us. If the pace has gotten too fast, then choose to slow down by taking a walk outside in the fresh air.

31 Change is like an ocean. When you are at sea, you can choose the direction of your course. You may have to fight the waves, maneuver around land barriers, and avoid collisions, but you can alter your direction at any given moment. You have no boundaries. So, chart your course by having a project plan—one that includes specific milestones to achieve. Be watchful for changes in the currents by knowing what is within the scope of the project. And finally, be ready to make small course corrections as you proceed on the journey.

32 ACCEPT THE UNCHANGEABLE. **Quit wasting time trying to Change the Unchangeable.** When it is your call, don't spend too much energy trying to change things that aren't worth the time and effort...Don't implement a $100 solution for a $50 problem!

33 CHANGE THE UNACCEPTABLE. If something doesn't "feel right," then go with your instincts. Ask yourself these questions:

- Do I want to change the situation in order to improve circumstances?
- Do I want to help people change so they will grow and advance?
- Once the change is implemented, will it make for better conditions for both me and those around me?
- Do I anticipate a return on my investment of time and money after the change is implemented?

If you answered YES to all of these questions, then DO IT! If you can't answer YES to all of these questions, then you probably need to rethink why you want to make the change.

Do not brace for change, but rather embrace change.

34 Timing is everything. Unfortunately with change, timing can make or break companies and individuals. The problem with implementing change is that it may never be the PERFECT time, but you need to perceive it as being the RIGHT time. Buy a watch or clock to leave on your desk, and put a tag on it that says "NOW is the right time for change."

35 We worry about life. Life is change. With change comes worry. It is a vicious cycle. Worry is like the dog that is constantly chasing his tail. He just runs 'round and 'round, never advancing, never progressing. Put a sign in your work area that says...STOP CHASING YOUR TAIL WITH WORRY!

Change   Worry

Life

36 Behave your way into a different perspective on change. Take some initiative. Empower yourself to look for ways of improving by identifying two things that could be done differently in your job this week, and GO FOR IT!

37 When change is implemented, your attitude and demeanor will be a positive or negative influence to all of those around you. Every day give yourself an *Attitude Check* asking: "Am I open to considering the benefits of change? Am I imagining the worst outcome instead of the best outcome? Am I prepared to be a problem solver versus a problem finder?"

Get beyond the pain to focus on the gain.

38 CREATE A QUIET PLACE! During times of change, people need their space. Sometimes it feels like the walls are closing in. Find a place in your company, department, or even at home, that allows you to get away and think things through. A quiet place, where you can enjoy a few private moments, is a godsend...and a great attitude adjuster.

39 Change takes dedicated time...Use your time wisely. Spend the first hour of the week planning and reviewing tasks in order to develop new skills. Ensure you've allocated the proper amount of time for change-related activities. Good planning can reduce stress, and reduced stress typically results in improved outlooks.

40 SUCCESS IS FAILURE TURNED INSIDE OUT. The next time you feel that you have failed at something, turn it into a success. Perhaps it is just a lesson learned, but use that knowledge to journey on to the next success. When you find yourself complaining about what failed, write the failure down, and then write down one way to overcome the failure.

You cannot succeed unless you try, and you cannot fail unless you try to succeed.

41 PLAN FOR THE UNEXPECTED. It is inevitable that along with change will come interruptions throughout your day. Therefore, plan for them by setting aside a block of time at the end of the day to deal with such matters.

42 DON'T REINVENT THE WHEEL! Although goals and processes may change, the skills and approaches needed to implement them may not. Analyze each change you face and ask yourself, "What have I learned, done, and applied successfully in the past that I can use to meet this new challenge?" Creating a plan to do things differently does not necessarily have to start with a blank sheet of paper. The more you can use what you've already mastered, the more positive your perspective on change will likely be.

43 Do it NOW! There may be no tomorrow to do what you want today. Therefore, LIVE today and PLAN for tomorrow.

44 Change was here YESTERDAY. Think of all the change you have been through in life, such as riding a bike your first time, learning your first sport, going to a new school, getting married, having children, losing a loved one, or starting a new job. Change has always been a part of your life. Make a list of ten changes in your life in the past five years. Spend a few minutes reflecting on how you felt when things were happening versus how you feel now. Would you consider most of these changes positive?

45 Change remains with us TODAY. As you live each day, you will continue to experience change. For lunch or dinner, choose to go to a different restaurant. Or if you do go to the same restaurant, order something that you have not tried before.

46 Change will continue TOMORROW. The next time you go to work, take a different route or a different type of transportation such as a bus or train. As you take the new route, make a mental note of three things you have not noticed before.

What happened in your past defines you, but where you are headed is what makes you.

47 Eliminate the clutter! Change can create chaos. Avoid a sense of being overwhelmed by keeping one task in front of you at a time. Constantly shifting through files and paperwork is a waste of valuable time. If you don't need it...TOSS IT!

48 Here is a lesson in *Human Nature 101:* When dealing with change, behaviors that get reinforced get repeated. Reward yourself whenever you successfully implement a change. That will increase the likelihood that you'll want to engage in similar behaviors in the future.

49 Find a diversion...at work. Identify an activity that will help you take a quick five or ten-minute break from work such as cleaning your workspace, organizing your files, taking a short walk, etc. Many successful companies have recreation areas or workout centers that host activities such as darts or Foosball. It allows workers to get away for a few minutes to "decompress" and come back a few minutes later much more invigorated.

50 Turn waiting time into learning time. Always keep reading materials on hand so that you can learn about new ideas or different ways of doing things while waiting for meetings and appointments. You'll likely find that increasing your exposure to new ideas and strategies will make the prospect of change less daunting.

51 Make New Year's Resolutions ALL YEAR. Changes in your personal life and goals in your professional life shouldn't only be reviewed once a year. Put a recurring task on your calendar on the 1st day of every month to "Examine changes I need to make."

52 WRITE A STORY. If you are having trouble with changes that are occurring, create a story with characters that fit the individuals being affected by the change. As you write the short story, write dialog from each character's point of view. It will help you see how the change affects everybody on the team, and it may help you look at things very differently.

53 Familiarity is reassuring and comforting. When going through a physical move, hold onto things that are familiar. Take an "icon," such as team pictures, your favorite chair, or old signage from the old location and place it in the new location.

54 RUN THE RACE! Often, it isn't a matter of "if" you will fall, but rather "when" you will fall. During changing times, obstacles will cross your path. Just ask yourself, "What will I do with these obstacles?" And most importantly...DON'T STOP RUNNING!

Welcome new ideas.
You never know where they may lead.

GET WITH IT:
WORKING WITH OTHERS THROUGH CHANGE

There could be change...There should be change...There WILL be change...Therefore, prepare yourself and other people for change. IT IS INEVITABLE! Preparing for change means that you have to be willing to take risks and work with people. Stop fearing what might happen. What would you do if you weren't afraid? You would TAKE RISKS!

When people are unhappy with their lives, what is the first thing they seek? Change! Ironic, huh? Change is required for self-preservation. Have you ever started a new job? Wasn't that change? Why did you change jobs? We constantly hear people say change is a negative topic in their life, yet people will change jobs in a heartbeat to "go to greener pastures."

The greater the difficulty, the more glory in surmounting it. Skillful pilots gain their reputation from storms and tempests.
- Epicurus

They do not have a fear of where they are going, but rather a determination to leave the current situation. People and companies can't have progress without change, so start changing TODAY! And here's how...

55 FIND A CHANGE BUDDY. You are part of the solution, or you have become part of the problem. Which are YOU? Ask someone to be your change partner. When you see each other creating more problems than solutions, keep one another accountable for your actions.

56 Actions DO speak louder than words. When communicating, 93% of people will respond to nonverbal signs over verbal communication. As you are delivering news of a changing situation, do a mental check as to how your body is responding. In addition, pay attention to other people's body language.

People may doubt what you say,
but they will believe what you do.

57 DON'T LIVE IN THE PAST! You CANNOT turn the clock back, so move on. Encourage people to stop talking about how things "used to be," and start talking about how things are "gonna be."

58 HAVE A *"THIS IS OUR LIFE PARTY."* When it is time to change things up within your life or organization, have a party where the people involved bring pictures, tell stories, and share memorabilia. Dedicate a huge bulletin board or wall, with an accompanying table, where people can post their items. It can help others see that changes over time help us evolve into where we are today.

59 Afraid of what? People aren't afraid of change, they are just afraid of the UNKNOWN. If we didn't have unknowns, then there would be no tomorrow. Every day is full of unknowns. Quit viewing the unknowns as a threat, and start viewing the unknowns as an adventure. Map out the change that is occurring. Then write a Risk Assessment that will identify the fears, threats, and their possible point of entry into the process. Turn it into a contest to "Conquer Gremlins" that stand in the way. Offer a prize to the person, or team, that conquers the most Gremlins.

60 Encourage people to remove negative words from their vocabulary. For example, take out the word CAN'T. Post these signs on the door of every cubicle and office in your department.

61 LEAD, FOLLOW, OR GET OUT OF THE WAY! You can choose to lead others to new opportunities; you can choose to follow your leader in advancing forward; or you need to move aside to let others evolve into something greater. When people are interfering with progress, ask them to kindly get out of the way.

62 Life isn't just "vanilla." Wouldn't life be boring if we were all the same...working the same jobs, driving the same cars, wearing the same clothes, going to the same schools, receiving the same degrees? You can't have change without having diversity. BE DIVERSE! Choose a day where people bring in their favorite flavors of ice cream or their favorite toppings. During an afternoon break, have a *Sundae Change* event.

63 RECOGNIZE OTHERS' EFFORTS. When you see others making positive strides toward implementing changes that are in the best interest of the team, recognize them by sending an e-mail or mentioning it during a team meeting.

64 DON'T SHOOT THE MESSENGER! Remember that many times during organizational change, the one to deliver the news of change is not the one that decided to make the change. If you are the one delivering the message, wear a banner that says "Don't Shoot the Messenger." It may lighten the burden.

65 DIFFERENCES DO MATTER! It is okay to have different opinions and outlooks—that is what makes the world go 'round. But are you willing to examine other people's ideas, and look beyond your own world? Put a Post-It note on your bathroom mirror that reads:

NOTE
Did I listen to someone else today?

66 Change comes in varying degrees. Depending on people's personalities, they handle change at different levels and intensities. Some people can be the *King or Queen of Change.* For those who are apprehensive about it, help them change in smaller degrees. Don't look at the entire piece of change that is occurring. Help them take their tasks and break them down into smaller pieces.

67 Doubt is a luxury you cannot afford. When moments of doubt slip into your mind, push them out. Change can be stifled because people start doubting their capabilities, or someone starts doubting the outcome before the task is under way. If you believe in something, there is no room for doubt.

Change is the essence of life. Be willing to surrender what you are for what you could become.
- Anonymous

68 Under the stress that often comes with change, resistance can lead to increased disagreement and strife on the team. Therefore, AGREE TO AGREE. Find one person that you rarely agree with. Sit in a room together, and don't leave until you each agree to agree with the other person. Pick up to ten topics that you disagree on and write them on a board or flipchart. Discuss each item until you can agree on at least two things. Not only will it help you manage through the change process, it will definitely improve your negotiation skills and team building abilities.

69 DON'T BE THE PUNCHING BAG...BUY ONE INSTEAD. Put a punching bag and a set of gloves in your office. When people get upset or angry with you or a situation, invite them to punch the bag.

70 Perception is the beholder's reality. It is easy to say that someone else is incorrect in how he or she views a certain situation or circumstance. However, that does not make you right and the other person wrong...it only means opinions matter. Make posters that say "Opinions Matter" and post them around the department, in the bathroom, in the lunchroom, and in other common areas that your team frequents. That will help everyone be more open and accepting of change.

71 STOP THE WHINING! Nobody likes to hear a complainer. When change has become inevitable, complaining becomes wasted energy. Tell people to take that energy and channel it toward improving the situation.

72 Don't allow fear to get in your way of success. The greatest detriment you can have to your well-being is to allow others to see your fear, or to allow them to bring you into "their misery."

Don't let other people spread their fears.

73 Prioritize for change. You will not have enough time to take care of everything that comes along during transitional periods. Therefore, make sure you help other people prioritize and take care of the things that matter most. Start a priority list and arrange it in High, Medium, and Low. Complete the High priorities before progressing to the Medium and then the Low.

74 Periodically remind yourself that with change comes transition, NOT instant gratification. There can't be change without a transition period. It may be a short period, or it may be a long and extended period. Make change deliberate. This is the time to stop doing things the way you used to do them, notice that there is a better way of doing them, and take time to implement the plan to do it differently in the future. **It can't change overnight!**

75 Ask the RIGHT questions. The quickest way to get different answers is to ask different questions. Change the types of questions you are asking...keep them open-ended.

76 BREAK THE CYCLE. Whenever you hear someone make a negative comment, point out the positive outcome from the change that is occurring.

If you change your attitude, you can change anything!

77 Help others see the *Big Picture.* The best way to get your point across is to draw it out in a visual form, such as a drawing, a flow chart, a project plan, etc. Make change visually stimulating.

78 Walk awhile in someone else's shoes. Find someone that you don't agree with, and figuratively change shoes with this person by exchanging a personal object for a day, such as a ring, watch, pen, or notepad. As issues arise throughout the day, let the item be a reminder of how the other person would respond to the situation, instead of how you would respond.

79 People who are not willing to change their minds CANNOT CHANGE anything. Therefore, to help people deal with change, help them change their minds by walking them through a list of pros and cons. Make the items as specific and personal as possible. Make sure they consider both the short-term and long-term impact. The impact on individuals is usually just short-term. This can make it an "easier pill to swallow."

80 You can lead a horse to water, but you CAN'T make it drink. It is important that you point out all of the positives that occur to people when they are in a changing environment. You can help them to realize the necessity for change, and you can assist them in planning to cope with it. Every time someone tells you why you CAN'T do something, tell him or her one reason why you CAN.

81 Resistance isn't necessarily a bad thing. But, when you allow resistance to interfere with progress, it has a negative impact. Therefore, try to use resistance to stimulate conversations around possibilities and to identify personal roadblocks. Schedule a meeting or a time of reflection to put words to the resistance.

When everything seems to be going against you, remember that the airplane takes off against the wind.

82 Avoid telling people just what they WANT to hear. Make sure to tell them what they NEED to hear too. After having a discussion with someone, ask yourself if you were honest with your responses.

83 HAVE A *CHANGE LIBRARY.*   In your workspace, have a library of information that you can share with others when discussing change. Collect books, Internet articles, humorous cartoons, etc. that can be shared with others when you are helping them deal with change.

84 Don't overcommit to others. During changing times, it becomes easy to focus on the people that don't adapt to the change. This can cause you to overcommit to the apprehensive people. At the beginning of the week, make a spreadsheet with each team member's name in a row. Each time you make a commitment to one of them, place a checkmark next to that person's name. Each time you decline to assist in something, place an X. At the end of the week, check to see if you are overcommitting. If so, determine if any team members are taking too much of your time. Each week review the past week and the current week to see if you are getting better at committing within reason.

> *What lies behind us and what lies before us are tiny matters compared to what lies within us.*
> - Ralph Waldo Emerson

85 GO TO THE SOURCE! If you have heard that some people are upset about changes that are occurring, make sure you speak with them directly. Ask them if they are handling everything okay, and ask if there is anything you can do to assist them. Don't avoid them just because they might be upset. By avoiding them, you may be adding fuel to the fire.

86 WINNERS FLOCK TOGETHER! Winners surround themselves with winners who continuously succeed. Find at least two successful people to "hang around." Successful people can give you advice on how to implement change successfully.

87 Remember...ENCOURAGE THEM! When change is being implemented, understand it, take charge of it, and support others who are trying to progress.

88 Understand *your* change versus *others'* change. People often label change as a "BAAADDDD" thing. They are really labeling change they can't control as *bad*. However, change they can control is labeled as *good*. Pull everyone together and list ways the changes are going to benefit everyone.

89 BE A *QUICK CHANGE* ARTIST. Have a day where your team members change something about themselves every two hours. They can change their hairstyle, change from contacts to glasses, change jewelry, change their shoes, change clothes, etc. Then have a contest to see who can tell what has changed in each team member. Have a prize for the one person that notices the most changes throughout the day.

90 This could be your finest hour. When you see the opportunity to be involved in a changing environment, jump right in. It allows you to show your flexibility and to be an example for those that surround you.

91 Other people sometimes see things that you can't see. USE THEM! Their perspective might be better than yours. Take one of your respectable team members to lunch and ask this person to tell you, constructively, how he or she thinks things are going.

Adaptability is the test of true character.

92 DON'T TAKE IT PERSONALLY! When you are the cheerleader for change, you will be the one trying to help others cope; and you will be trying to rally the troops to move in the same direction. That's not an easy task...expect resistance along the way. *Remember, you are not the target, you just happen to be within firing range.*

93 "Failure is not an option." UNTRUE! Unfortunately, failure is always an option. When appropriate, remind other people that when they choose to do nothing, they are choosing to fail.

94 GIVE HIGH FIVES! When you notice that someone has easily adapted to a change, give this person a high five for taking it so well.

95 CLEAR UP AMBIGUITY! When you meet with people, don't let the "unknowns" become the focus of discussions. Make sure that you set things straight with your people, always keeping them in the loop. However, don't let them get sidetracked on what you cannot change.

> *When you are no longer able to change a situation, we are challenged to change ourselves.*
>
> - Viktor Frankl

96 HELP THEM GROW in order to help them change! Work with people to develop their talents and enhance their skills. When you put time, energy and resources into others' development, you not only recognize their potential, but you are setting everyone up for future success.

97 Is it decision time? When making decisions, take two pieces of paper. Write PROS on the top of one and CONS on the top of the other. Start listing the advantages and disadvantages of making the change. Determine a time limit, and once the time is up, review the list and make the decision!

98 Change can produce fear, which can make your department seem like a cloudy day. Always remember that behind the clouds, the sun is still shining. Don't allow others to be the darkness that overshadows the brightness. Put crepe paper banners on a fan in your department that say: "BLOW THE CLOUDS OF FEAR AWAY!"

99 WEAR YOUR FEELINGS ON YOUR SLEEVE. Supply white t-shirts and art supplies for the team members. Allow them to make their own t-shirt and wear it for the day. They can decorate the shirt however they like. On their sleeve, they need to write one thing that is good about the changes occurring.

100 If all else fails, tell other people to **GET OVER IT!** Change is part of life, and life must go on.

The greatest changes in life come at the most unexpected time.

GET TO IT:
LEADING CHANGE EFFECTIVELY

Leaders play a critical role when it comes to change. Whether you and your team are going through small daily changes or large organizational changes, you need to be able to help everyone cope with the changes that lie ahead. Remember that change is the foundation to organizational survival. Yesterday's success doesn't mean that tomorrow is secure. Therefore, you must be willing to change with the times.

Just because we have always done it "that" way, doesn't mean it will work the same way forever. If you're facing obstacles in implementing change, keep moving. It doesn't matter whether you go around them, over them, or under them, **just keep moving forward!**

Change isn't inherently *good*...Nor is it inherently *bad*...However, change will always be necessary for survival. Here are some useful ideas for those faced with leading others through change...

> *Men make history, and not the other way around. In periods where there is no leadership, society stands still. Progress occurs when courageous, skillful leaders seize the opportunity to change things for the better.*
>
> - Harry S. Truman

101 Be mentally prepared. When you are dealing with change and dealing with people that are affected by change, allow everyone time to get mentally prepared. In your initial conversations, describe the impending change—along with the reasons for it—and let everyone contemplate what is about to happen. Encourage people to sort out their mental and emotional feelings. Reconvene the next day to discuss the "nitty-gritty details" of what is about to occur.

102 LAUGH MORE! Change often creates tension within the team. As a leader, you must monitor the team, and create quick relief. Humor helps. At staff meetings, open by having one member of your team tell something humorous that recently happened.

103 Don't just manage...LEAD. There is no greater time to demonstrate your leadership skills than during times of change. Anyone can just manage a group of people, but it takes an extraordinary person to lead a team of people through a successful implementation of change. What is the difference? A *manager* would take the "this is the way it is" approach by assigning tasks, stating deadlines, and taking the "get it done" approach. However, a *leader* must have compassion, understanding, organization skills, communication skills, and be able to see the end result before you actually get there.

> ### *Leaders see the invisible,*
> ### *believe the incredible,*
> ### *and do the impossible.*

104 People have different tolerance levels when it comes to dealing with change. You need to acknowledge that not all people can handle the same amount at once. Some people can handle large degrees of change, and they may even thrive on the excitement of change. Others may have to be dealt change in small doses. Know your own tolerances first, and then be able to identify those of your work group. Once you have identified how each individual deals with change, start assigning tasks accordingly. For example, if one team member tends to like change, then you might put this person in a *change leadership* position when a new task is assigned to your team.

105 Cushion the bad news with some good news. Tell employees many of the positive things happening in your organization and work groups before you tell them about the change that is going to take place.

106 Change is like a puzzle. Get together with everyone affected by the change, and create a puzzle. Cut out all of the pieces of the puzzle, and write the tasks that must occur in order for the puzzle to be finished in the end. Assign pieces to people, and when they are finished with their task, have them add their piece to the puzzle board.

107 One month after you have implemented change, pull your team together. Give them 60 seconds to write down three things that "used to be." You will be amazed that the new way seems more "normal" to people, and some might even struggle to remember three things.

108 KNOW THE DEGREES OF CHANGE. Change is good, but too much change, too fast, can be devastating. Therefore, be aware of the facts. Know how much change can take place in a given amount of time without sinking your ship! Here are some good indicators that too much change is happening too quickly or that things are out of control:

- Increased absenteeism.
- Continual conflict between team members.
- Turnover of team members.
- Decreased productivity.
- Increase in mistakes being made.

109 You can't lead a change initiative if you are the last one to know what's happening in your organization and your work group. You can't solve problems if you are not aware of them. Make sure that you have open lines of communication with all of your team members. Do a *Monday Morning Walkabout*. Walk around the common areas of your department or building. Spend time asking people about their weekend, what their focus for the week is going to be, and how you can assist them in the upcoming week.

110 **When change is needed, the greatest risk is doing nothing at all.** By doing nothing, you will constantly be focusing on what you don't have in life, and never be able to focus on what you could have in life. The next time your team is facing change, ask yourself, "As the leader, am I doing everything I can to make the transition go smoothly?"

Sometimes you must climb out on a limb in order to get the best fruit.

111 GET PHYSICAL! If you are debating over which of two equally beneficial options to select, find a tangible way to make the decision...thumb wrestle...play rock-paper-scissors...flip a coin...draw straws...pick a number out of a hat.

112 Operate with clearly defined SMART (Specific, Measurable, Attainable, Realistic, Time bound) goals and objectives. You will get the best mileage out of your people. Tell them what you expect...Review with them as you go...Summarize with them once you arrive. Create a *SMART Bulletin Board* with your team. Add an area for short-term goals and another area for long-term goals.

113 Monitor your team's temperature. Once a week, have a short, informal "How are things going?" chat with each person who reports to you. And pay attention to how team members behave and interact with one another—especially when working on tasks and projects that involve change. If you sense that things aren't right, investigate each potential problem and take whatever action is appropriate to "nip it in the bud."

114 During organizational changes, watch for any unusual behaviors. Notice how people are reacting by watching their body language, listening for differences in tones of voice or gestures, watching to see if they are isolating themselves from the team, and being aware of increased whispering or closed doors. These all might be signs of people's fear of change and of the unknowns.

> *Nothing can be done without hope and confidence.*
> - Helen Keller

115 CREATE A DREAM TEAM! You can't reach a "10" dream with a "2" team attitude. View organizational change as a personal challenge. Make a *Dream Team Chart* where you have two columns: STRENGTHS and CHALLENGES (Weaknesses). Write down each member's top three strengths and three greatest challenges in the corresponding columns. Draw a line between one team member's strength that offsets another team member's weakness. Try to match as many challenges and strengths as possible. If you find items that don't match, the next team member you add should have the strengths to offset these challenges.

116 LET 'EM SPEAK! Encourage full participation and disclosure during times of change. Use a Koosh ball in your meetings. Toss it around the room, and establish a rule that people must have the ball in order to speak. Let each person ask one question, and give two minutes for the response and open discussion before proceeding to the next question. *Hint: Use a stopwatch.* This allows your entire team to participate, and it breaks tension because many times laughter will result from how people are throwing or catching the ball.

117 Have a *Change Gripe Jar.* If people want to just gripe about the change that is occurring, have them write it down and put it in the Gripe Jar. Tally the results. Tell them what can and can't be addressed and why. Give them a plan with a timeline to get back to them, and then take those that are not actionable and host a shredding party.

Top 10 Excuses for NOT Changing
...with counter objections

1	*"We have always done it this way."* Just because it was successful in the past, doesn't necessarily mean it's the best way now... or that it will be in the future.
2	*"We have not done that before."* At one time, <u>everything</u> we do now was something we had never done before.
3	*"We tried that before and failed."* Unless all conditions and circumstances are exactly the same, failure of the past should not dictate our successes of the future.
4	*"If it isn't broke, let's not fix it."* Change doesn't mean it's broken, it only means we need to improve it.
5	*"It's too much trouble."* The greatest rewards in life usually take the most time and energy.
6	*"It's too expensive, and we just can't afford it."* You can't afford not to! You must spend money to make money.
7	*"It will just change again soon."* It may change tomorrow, or it might not change for some time. Regardless, our fears of the need to keep changing should never prevent us from doing so.
8	*"I like it the way it is."* It may be <u>good</u> the way it is, but it could be <u>great</u> the new way. Besides, if we never moved away from what we like, we all might still be riding horses to work!
9	*"I may not be needed after the change."* With change comes a time to grow. This may be your chance to do new and exciting things.
10	*"It's too risky."* The greatest rewards always come with the greatest risk.

118 SILENCE IS GOLDEN...USE IT. When you make an announcement that dramatically affects a team of people, give 60 seconds of silence for it to sink in. Before you proceed, let them decipher the information and formulate their questions.

119 YELL A CHEER! It is a test of resilience. Anybody can be a cheerleader when things are going right. It is when things are going wrong that measures an individual's true leadership qualities.

120 Have a *Do Over Party* after implementing organizational change. Have a lunch gathering that you sponsor to celebrate what people learned—good and bad—during the times of change! Ask all of your team members what they would do the same and what they would do differently if they had the chance to go through the same change again.

121 Don't plant seeds in untilled soil! Just as in nature, the seeds of organizational change need to be planted in soil that has been prepared to accept the germinating ideas. So, involve others in the planning and cultivating of ideas. The ground has to be fertilized with rich additives, so supply information outlining the good business reasons for the change.

122 WATCH TURNOVER. During times of organizational change and uncertainty, the most talented people often are the first to leave the organization. Avoid this by making them a part of the solution. Delegate higher levels of responsibilities to your key people, and make them your "go to people."

123 **Have a TACO day.** Each member of the team must bring in one ingredient to effectively make a taco: shells, meat, lettuce, tomatoes, onions, cheese, salsa, etc. The focus of the day is that each ingredient by itself cannot make a taco. However, once you combine the items, you can effectively create an awesome TACO—**T**eams **A**ccept **C**hanging **O**pportunities.

124 Change your clothes. On the rollout day of a new project, have a day where people wear clothes that are not their normal attire. For example, a sports theme day, casual day, or a costume day.

125 DRAW A LINE IN THE CONFERENCE ROOM. At your next important decision-making meeting, place masking tape down the center of the room, dividing it in half. Put a sign on one half that says GO and a sign on the other half that says NO GO. Have the participants choose which side of the decision they are on. Start your discussions, and have people freely move between the sides of the room based on their input. Once you have a certain percentage on a specific side, your decision is made!

126 PLAY THE GAME. During times of stressful reorganizations, put a Foosball table, Ping-Pong table, or a basketball hoop in the employee lunch area. Organize a daily play-off between teams or departments. This will allow teams of people to relieve stress in a friendly and competitive manner.

127 DON'T FOCUS ON THE STRESS. Studies repeatedly show that organizational change dramatically increases the level of job stress for employees. Remember to FOCUS ON THE GOAL. Buy stress balls for everyone that say "Focus on the Goal."

128 **Take one for the team.** If your team has made a mistake and you are called on the carpet, DON'T BLAME OTHERS...INSTEAD TAKE THE BLAME. Your team will respect you for it.

129 GET OUT YOUR BOOM BOX! People can tense up and retreat to their own workspaces in times of change. Occasionally put your boom box outside your office and play a couple of dance songs, such as YMCA, Electric Slide, Locomotion, or the Chicken Dance. It will energize the team and get people out of their cubicles.

130 CHANGE IT UP! Help your team get accustomed to frequent changes. Every once in a while, have each team member exchange one object in his or her cubicle (chair, mouse pad, monitor, portfolio, favorite pen, etc.) with another team member for one week.

131 Integrity is the grandfather of honesty. Being honest isn't all it takes to effectively lead through change. You must also do what you say you will do...or in other words, **WALK THE TALK!**

Your job title is a label. Leader is a position.

132 Remain the same during moves. When you are going through a location change, keep people within their comfort zone. For example, keep them in the same seating pattern, same furniture, same chair, etc.

133 RING THE BELL! To encourage your team in times of change, hang a bell in your department where everyone can hear it. When a member of the team has a success that involves some degree of change, allow this person to ring the bell. For example, in a sales department, ring the bell if a sale of an increased amount is made. Or in a customer service department, ring the bell if you reached a new daily goal of incoming calls.

134 Mix up your team by playing musical chairs. Next time you are in an all day meeting or training session, make people randomly walk around the room while you play a CD. When the music stops, make them sit in the nearest chair for the rest of the day.

135 KEEP THE CHANGE! At the beginning of a project, give each team member a roll of coins (nickels, dimes, or quarters) in a baggie. The higher the value...the better. Each time people complain to other team members, they are required to give the person they are complaining to a coin. At the end of the project, have a grand prize for the person who has the most original coins left (meaning this person complained the least). Everyone else gets to "keep the change" in his or her baggie.

136 Change is exploring OTHER possibilities, not always exploring the SAME ones. At the end of every month, ask yourself, "What can my team do differently next month to make us more productive and efficient?"

You cannot have REWARDS without RISK.

137 Allow the student to become the teacher. Proactively listen to your subordinates. Ask them, "What would you do if you were on this side of the desk?" **LISTEN...AND LEARN.**

138 Change the importance of change by focusing on it. Add a *Change Line Item* to your agenda for the next department meeting. Ask for input from your team about what changes, whether big or small, you can make to improve your department, your projects, your environment, your productivity, etc.

LETTER TO AN EMPLOYEE

Dear Employee:

I know that times are changing, which means uncertainty about the future. However, remember that we cannot get to where we are going, unless we are willing to take a journey.

There are many days I feel the same as you...wanting everything to stay the same...allowing me to stay in my comfort zone...not wanting to get out of my box. I need to stop looking at this moment in time as "me" and start looking at it as "we." I must learn to look beyond my own desires to see what is in the best interest of the organization, which also means in the best interest of "us." If we are willing to change, evolve, and grow with ABC Company, then we will all succeed...Together!

Think of this time of organizational change as a time that we can experience new things, and perhaps move in new directions—ones that we never knew existed—allowing us to be more effective, more efficient, and more energized.

Thank you for all of your support over the years, and I am sure we can make it through these changing times together.

Sincerely,

Your Manager

139 Change can surface emotional responses, so make sure that you demonstrate empathy. Learn to use two very powerful words, "I understand." It doesn't necessarily mean you agree. However, it does state that you understand what they are saying. It can diffuse confrontations very quickly.

140 Give a ten-minute oil change. When things are stressful, allow people ten minutes to just "squeak" and get things off their chest. Just listen...don't respond until their ten minutes are up. Once their ten minutes are up, discuss the situation, and explore things they can do to overcome any difficulties they may be facing.

141 LIFE IS CHANGE. CHANGE IS LIFE! All areas of life are going to change: your age, schools, jobs, responsibilities, family, spouses, children, homes, churches, cars, etc. Make sure people know THAT'S LIFE! When people challenge you as a leader on the subject of change, ask them to tell you about the last time they made a personal change in order to enhance their lives. Then explain that organizations are the same as people. They have to change in order to progress.

> *Progress is impossible without change, and those who cannot change their minds cannot change anything.*
> - George Bernard Shaw

142 TAKE A BREATHER! As long as your employees' anxiety and level of concern remains at a reasonable limit, you can use it to motivate. Nervous energy can be a positive thing, just make sure to help them channel it in the right direction. When you see an employee's anxiety level getting beyond "reasonable," have the person "take a breather" by assigning a small task that will take the mind off the current situation.

143 Give credit where credit is due. Next time you receive a compliment on your department from a "higher authority," ask the person to e-mail a thank you note to the people that completed the change-related task.

144 Conduct *Temperature Check Surveys*. Have a pre-mid-post survey that people complete during projects that involve change. Ask rated questions (i.e. 1 to 10) regarding progress, environment, stress levels, etc. Give short comment sections for them to also give you quick feedback. Compare the results throughout the process. It can help you alter things as you go.

145 Avoid the rumor mill. Emphasize the importance of holding confidential information and not believing what team members hear "through the grapevine." Take a flipchart, and turn it away from the people. Write a long and complex sentence with approximately 25 words. Whisper the sentence into the ear of the person next to you. Have the person whisper it to the person next to him or her, and so on until each person has been told the sentence. Don't allow people to repeat the sentence or to ask any questions. Have the last person say what he or she heard. Turn the flipchart and read the original sentence. Then make the point that the grapevine can distort a message...DRAMATICALLY. This will help everyone understand why clear communication is essential during change.

146 KEEP YOUR FINGER ON THE PULSE! In order to effectively manage change, you must always know where you have been, where you are in the process, and where you are headed. Create a timeline on the wall, and create Post-It notes that have tasks or goals. Then put the Post-It notes under the proper categories. Under Past, list what you have finished; under Present, list what you are working on; and under Future, list your outstanding items.

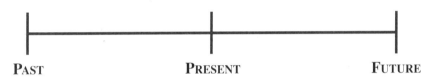

PAST   PRESENT   FUTURE

147 Guidance from you as a leader helps keep your people focused and on track. People want to follow someone. Remember this: If you are not leading them, they will find someone else to follow. Ask yourself, "Are my people following through on my communications with them?"

148 *KUDOS TO ALL.* Create a *Kudos Board* where team members can post positive comments about other team members.

149 Conduct a *Now What?* brainstorming session. Get your team together at the first of the year and make goals of what can be successfully changed this year.

150 IT'S MAGIC DAY! Hire a magician to come in and perform. After the performance, have a discussion about how your mind "perceives" something that is nonexistent. This is how change can be. We can worry about things that are not even there. Therefore, look behind the "magic curtain."

151 **KNOW YOUR STUFF WITHOUT STRUTTING YOUR STUFF.** No one likes a show-off. People are attracted to people with confidence, not people with arrogance. Periodically ask yourself, "Do my people see me as friend or foe...and what makes me think so?"

152 Be upbeat and positive. You are your best cheerleader. "It isn't if you win or lose, but it is how you play the game." If your team is losing the game, you still have to cheer them on. If you stop cheering, your team just may stop trying.

153 Examine *Lessons Learned.* After you or your team completes a task or project, ask yourself, "What did we do right? What did we do wrong?" Make a document, and save the information to enhance and improve your future performance.

154 Avoid negative returns by making sure the ultimate cost of the solution is less than the cost of the problem. Do a cost-benefit analysis report that justifies the change and have the key people sign off on the document.

155 Have a *Change Cuss Bucket* to avoid statements such as "We've tried that before" or "That's not the way we do that here." Every time people use a negative statement about the situation, or make a derogatory comment about a team member, make them put a dollar in the bucket. During the December holidays, donate the money to a family in need.

156 The change process works in a strange way. The solution of one problem can actually create more problems. Don't be alarmed when this occurs. Break the problems down. Make a plan of action for each situation, and make sure to assign the right team members to solving the right problems.

157 GIVE 'EM SPACE. Hanging over people and micromanaging will create tension that is counterproductive to positive change.

158 Have a **F**ocus **O**n **O**thers **D**ay. Work on projects with other people for the entire day. Rotate around team members to accomplish small tasks. On that day, have everyone bring in favorite snack foods.

159 PULL 'EM OUT! When it comes time to implement change, some people will put their heads in the sand. When you see people struggling with change, pull them out of their environment for a quick coffee break and ask them how they are doing. Find out how you can help them deal with the changes that are occurring.

160 KICK 'EM OUT! If pulling their head out of the sand doesn't work, then kick them out. Change is most effective when you have buy-in from the team. You don't need negative team members bringing you down. If you can't get someone to be a positive contributor, then try to get that person off your project or off your team.

161 BE A HANDYMAN! When you see one of your team members struggling with implementing something new in his or her job, offer to lend a helping hand to get this person started on the right track. You probably have "tools" in your toolkit of experience that your team members would find very useful.

162 PLANT A TREE OF CHANGE. If you are put in charge of a new department or division during a large organizational restructure, donate a tree, and as a team, plant it on the company grounds. It will be a reminder of how you have grown together through the organizational change.

People are like trees.
If they bend with the wind, they will survive.
If they have rigid limbs, they snap off during the storm.

163 Put a *Change Machine* in your department. This is a locked suggestion box where people can submit ideas of things they think would be a positive change. Allow them to submit any ideas and to submit them anonymously. Review the box on a regular basis, and at your staff meetings, read at least one of the changes that you have decided to implement.

164 THESE WILL BE "THE GOOD OLE DAYS"!! Keep telling your team that everything happens for a reason, and remember that some day we will look back on these days of change as "The Good Ole Days."

Don't dwell on the past, only look to the future,
but don't forget to live in your present.

165 HAVE A DRINK...AT WORK! When you have successfully completed a project that required the team to implement a lot of change, bring in Sparkling Cider, plastic Champagne flutes, and some snacks. TOAST to your success before going home for the weekend.

166 RAISE THE BAR. Don't allow your team to always accomplish the same things, the same way, and in the same amount of time. The best leaders in the world will make their people stretch. Help your team to realize that they can do things better, faster, and more efficiently. Nail a limbo bar to the wall of your department with different peg heights. As you get closer to your goal, and you reach measurable milestones, keep raising the bar one peg at a time, until your team reaches the top peg.

167 Make a *Mission Board* when change is being implemented. On the board, create a battlefield or firing range, and put the targets that need to be hit in order for the mission to be accomplished. As each target or battle is finished, remove it from the *Mission Board*. Once all items have been completed or eliminated, have a "We Won the Battle" party.

168 GIVE 'EM THE FACTS! If you expect people to support significant organizational change, you have to give them the "straight scoop" on things like your organization's financial picture and the real impact of some new business competition. Only confidential information should be kept secret.

169 BE THE BOSS FOR A DAY. If you are having trouble getting buy-in from your team during an organizational change, let them (as a team) be the boss for a day. Let them spend a day figuring out how they would handle things if they were in charge. Make a list of the suggestions. Implement what makes sense and tell people why!

170 Learn what MOTIVATES your people. Contrary to popular belief, money is NOT the #1 motivator. People can be motivated by many things, such as recognition, rewards, praise, new assignments, food, extracurricular activities, time off, etc. Don't motivate them based on what motivates you. Motivate them based on what motivates THEM. Keep a handbook of people's favorite hobbies, restaurants, types of movies, family members, family activities, etc. Next time you want to reward someone or give a gift, take an item from your handbook and make it the focus of the reward.

171 SMILE...YOU'RE ON CAMERA! Before a major physical change takes place (location move, reorganization of people, dress code change, new office furniture, decorating an office, etc.), take before and after pictures. Hang them up or put them in your company scrapbook as a display that change can be positive.

172 Create a *Change Success Book* for your team. As your team effectively implements changes that are successful to the organization, they can write their success in the book. They can fill the book with pictures, memos, stories, etc. It should focus on changes they implemented that have had a positive and successful impact on the organization.

173 Sometimes change can be life changing to those impacted. When you have to be the bearer of bad news, meet in a neutral territory such as a conference room or a coffee shop. This makes the meeting less threatening to other people.

174 CHANGE IT UP! Don't always allow your employees to do things the same way over and over again. Change it up every once in a while by throwing them a curve ball. For example, if they are always used to sitting in the same seat at staff meetings, give them ten seconds to change to a different seat, not sitting next to the same person. Sometimes helping people adjust to small changes in their lives allows them to adjust to larger changes more easily.

175 At least once a month, go searching for the BAD NEWS. You would rather know the bad news before anyone else does. This allows you the opportunity to cut it off at the pass. Don't put your earplugs in, trying to avoid what your team is saying. Go searching, and ask your employees to tell you three things that are wrong and need to be fixed. Then, start fixing what you can. And along the same line...

176 THE LEAKY PIPE! If it's broken, then FIX IT! It may only be a drip now, but once the pipe bursts, your clean up will take a lot longer. Write down all the things that are broken in your team, and create a 90-day plan on how to fix the problems. Things have to change in order for progress to take place, so make the necessary changes.

177 Change is Progress, so make a *Slider Progress Bar* that is broken down into days, weeks, months, or years. As items are finished, allow members of the team to move the slider to the next time slot. Everyone can see the progress that your team is making.

WEEK 1	WEEK 2	WEEK 3	WEEK 4	WEEK 5	WEEK 6	WEEK 7	WEEK 8	WEEK 9	WEEK 10
			▲						

Progress is change. Change is progress.

178 FLEX IT! When you are going through large amounts of organizational change, consider allowing your employees to work flex-time schedules, even if on a short-term basis. This can help them to work a their maximum efficiency. For example, if you have morning people, they might be less stressed by getting in early and working through the issues, versus working late into the evening when they are not at their best.

179 People fear what they cannot see. Because so many people cannot see the "finish line," they decide not to join the race. Just because you are standing at the beginning of the *Race of Change*, you must remember there is a finish line. Even though you cannot see the ribbon at the other end, it still exists. In a race, this is where the largest part of the crowd is waiting! Create a racetrack in the hallways of your department, and place milestone signs of what needs to be accomplished, along with a "finish line," on the walls.

180 POST CHANGE...DON'T POSTPONE CHANGE! You can maximize the potential benefits of change by making a poster for your department that reminds you of the steps to implementing change effectively:

Commit to it

Harness it

Accept it

Notice it

Get with it

Embrace it

AND FINALLY...

You cannot have a future without change.

Remember that what you do today is what impacts the type of day you will have tomorrow. You have choices…you have perceptions…you have ideas…you have dreams…These are the fabrics of who you are. Start thinking today about how you want to impact tomorrow. You cannot do it without making the necessary changes, so start changing today!

> *I like dreams of the future better than the history of the past.*
> - Thomas Jefferson

The **past** was yesterday…leave it there!
Today is the **present**…live it!
Tomorrow is the **future**…plan for it!

ABOUT THE AUTHOR

Laurie Calzada is an entrepreneur, author, motivational speaker and trainer with almost 20 years of experience. She presents on many topics, such as leadership, mastering change, and sales. Her focus is to motivate those who have a desire to excel, and her life has proven that you can accomplish anything with enough determination and ambition. Her outstanding career has allowed her to consult and present for hundreds of Fortune 1,000 companies.

With an entrepreneurial spirit, she has successfully owned and founded seven different start-up operations over the past 20 years. Currently, she owns three companies. Dynamic Approach helps companies and employees find their "true passion" by evaluating core values of the organization, focusing on improving the cultural environment, and assisting management at all levels in coaching and mentorship skills. Sharp Approach is a technology-based business that specializes in sales force automation and CRM products. Sharp Connection is an ISP that offers data and website hosting to clients.

Ms. Calzada began her career 20 years ago while studying Marketing at the University of Maryland, European Division in Oxford, England. In addition, she received a certificate of Broadcast Journalism from the Broadcast Center. She is also the author of *Inspiring Passion in Others* and *Nine Principles to Living Your Life With Passion (coming 2007)*.

ABOUT THE PUBLISHER

Since 1977, The WALK THE TALK Company has helped organizations and individuals, worldwide, achieve success through Ethical Leadership and Values-Based Business Practices. And we're ready to do the same for you!

We offer a full range of proven resources and customized services—all designed to help you turn shared values like Integrity, Respect, Responsibility, Customer Service, Trust, and Commitment into workplace realities.

To learn more about the WALK THE TALK Company or to order additional copies of this high-impact handbook, call **888.822.9255** or visit **www.walkthetalk.com**.

You will discover our full range of products and services to include:

- Employee Development Tools
- Video Training Programs
- Motivational and Inspirational Gift Books
- "How To" Leadership Development Resources
- Keynotes and Conference Presentations
- Training Workshops and Consulting Services
- The popular *Santa's Leadership Secrets*™ and *Start Right...Stay Right* product lines
- *and much more!*

OTHER "180 TIPS" HANDBOOKS FROM

The WALK THE TALK Company

180 Ways to Build Commitment and Positive Attitudes
This NEW Walk The Talk handbook provides individuals and leaders with practical tools to turn attitudes into effective actions in a way that builds commitment to desired results. $9.95

180 Ways to Spread Contagious Enthusiasm
In this heartwarming handbook, best-selling author Barbara Glanz gives you 180 morale-boosting ideas to help you bring more kindness, communication, respect, and appreciation to your workplace. $9.95

180 Ways to Walk the Leadership Talk
This quick reference handbook includes 180 leadership tips and techniques to help current and future leaders shape an environment that attracts and retains the people you need and produces the results you want. $9.95

180 Ways to Walk the Motivation Talk
180 Ways to Walk the Motivation Talk is a practical, cost-effective guide for energizing your entire organization to achieve higher levels of collaboration, commitment, and productivity. $9.95

180 Ways to Walk the Customer Service Talk
Packed with powerful strategies and tips to cultivate world-class customer service, this handbook promises to be the answer to getting everyone "Walking the Customer Service Talk" and building a reputation of service integrity. $9.95

180 Ways to Walk the Recognition Talk
A powerful guide packed with ideas and suggestions for reinforcing good performance and creating a culture of appreciation. $9.95

180 Ways to Build a Magnetic Culture
This quick-reference handbook is filled with ideas, techniques, and strategies for retaining, attracting, and hiring the best, brightest, and most productive people. $9.95

ORDER FORM
Have questions? Need assistance? Call 1.888.822.9255

☑ **Please send me additional copies of 180 Ways to Effectively Deal with Change**
1-99 copies: $9.95 ea.   100-499 copies: $8.95 ea.   500+ copies: *call **1.888.822.9255***

180 Ways to Effectively Deal with Change_____ copies X $_____ = $_____

Additional Resources

180 Ways to Build Commitment
and Positive Attitudes _____ copies X $ 9.95 = $_____

180 Ways to Spread Contagious
Enthusiasm _____ copies X $ 9.95 = $_____

180 Ways to Walk the Leadership Talk _____ copies X $ 9.95 = $_____

180 Ways to Walk the Motivation Talk _____ copies X $ 9.95 = $_____

180 Ways to Walk the Customer
Service Talk _____ copies X $ 9.95 = $_____

180 Ways to Walk the Recognition Talk _____ copies X $ 9.95 = $_____

180 Ways to Build A Magnetic Culture _____ copies X $ 9.95 = $_____

Product Total $_____

(Sales & Use Tax Collected on TX & CA Customers Only)

* Shipping & Handling $_____

Subtotal $_____

Sales Tax:
TX Sales Tax – 8.25% $_____
CA Sales/Use Tax $_____
TOTAL (U.S. Dollars Only) $_____

*Shipping and Handling Charges							
No. of Items	1-4	5-9	10-24	25-49	50-99	100-199	200+
Total Shipping	$6.75	$10.95	$17.95	$26.95	$48.95	$84.95	$89.95+$0.25/book

Call 972.243.8863 for quote if outside continental U.S. Orders are shipped ground delivery 3–5 days.
Next and 2nd business day delivery available – call 1.888.822.9255.

Name_____ Title _____

Organization _____

Shipping Address No P.O. Boxes _____

City_____ State_____ Zip _____

Phone _____ Fax _____

E-Mail _____

Charge Your Order: ❑ MasterCard   ❑ Visa   ❑ American Express

Credit Card Number_____ Exp. _____

❑ Check Enclosed (Payable to: The WALK THE TALK Company)

❑ Please Invoice (Orders over $250 ONLY)   P.O. # (required) _____

Prices effective December 1, 2006 are subject to change.

PHONE
1.888.822.9255
or 972.243.8863
M-F, 8:30 – 5:00 Central

FAX
972.243.0815

ONLINE
www.walkthetalk.com

MAIL
WALK THE TALK CO.
2925 LBJ Fwy, #201
Dallas, TX 75234